Deregulation:

Where Do We Go from Here?

Deregulation:
Where Do We Go from Here?

Paul L. Joskow

The AEI Press

WASHINGTON, D.C.

Distributed to the Trade by National Book Network, 15200 NBN Way, Blue Ridge Summit, PA 17214. To order call toll free 1-800-462-6420 or 1-717-794-3800. For all other inquiries please contact the AEI Press, 1150 Seventeenth Street, N.W., Washington, D.C. 20036 or call 1-800-862-5801.

Library of Congress Cataloging-in-Publication Data

Joskow, Paul L.
  Deregulation : where do we go from here? / Paul L. Joskow.
      p. cm.
"2009 Reg-Markets Center Distinguished Lecture."
Includes bibliographical references.
    ISBN-13: 978-0-8447-4320-2 (pbk)
    ISBN-10: 0-8447-4320-8
    1. Deregulation—United States. 2. Trade regulation—United States
I. Title.

    HD3616.U47J67 2009
    338.973—dc22

                                                    2009030468

13 12 11 10 09   1 2 3 4 5

Printed in the United States of America

Contents

Foreword

The 2009 American Enterprise Institute Center for Regulatory and Market Studies Distinguished Lecture Award was given to Professor Paul L. Joskow. This award honors an individual who has made major contributions to the field of regulation and related areas. Senior members of the center select the distinguished lecturer on the basis of both scholarly achievement and practical contributions to the field. The lecturer has complete discretion in choosing the topic.

Professor Joskow is one of the world's leading scholars in applied economics. The areas of regulation and analysis of industrial organization that he has influenced are numerous. For example, Professor Joskow has done superb work on energy, on topics ranging from the economics of conservation, to electric utility restructuring, to the prospects for nuclear power.

My first encounter with his work was in a 1974 paper in the *Journal of Law and Economics* on the regulation of public utilities, in which he argued that the standard model used by economists for analyzing the behavior of regulators did not track real-world conditions. While nominally setting rates of return on invested capital, regulators actually set prices. Furthermore, regulators responded in predictable ways to political pressures. The analysis illustrated how empirical research could both inform our understanding of utility behavior and provide a framework for improving the design of regulatory policy.

In addition to his seminal work on economic regulation, Professor Joskow has done path-breaking research on market-based approaches to containing pollution. When the allowance trading regime for sulfur emissions was implemented in 1995, no one was certain how it would work. The government is, of course, a major player in this synthetic market, and, in theory, government could structure it to maximize efficiency. But the question was how the market would work in practice. Professor Joskow, in collaboration with colleagues at MIT, put theory to the test. Their analysis has stood the test of time well, providing important insights into the design of market-based approaches for containing greenhouse gas emissions.

Professor Joskow has also made important contributions to our understanding of how considerations of transactions costs affect the organization of firms, the structure and performance of contractual relationships among firms, and the factors that lead firms to integrate vertically both to reduce costs and to enhance market power. He has also analyzed how such considerations should affect the design of efficient antitrust and regulatory policies.

Professor Joskow has received many awards for his scholarly work. He was elected a fellow of the Econometric Society and of the American Academy of Arts and Sciences. He is a distinguished fellow of the Industrial Organization Society; he received the Lifetime Achievement Award of the International Association for Energy Economics, the Adelman-Frankel Award of the United States Society for Energy Economics for "unique and innovative contributions to the field of energy economics," served as president of the International Society for New Institutional Economics, was awarded an honorary doctorate by the University of Paris-Dauphine, and has received other honors and awards. He was also elected to membership on the Council on Foreign Relations. In 2008, he became president of the Alfred P. Sloan Foundation, a philanthropic institution focused on research and broad-based education in science, technology, and economic performance.

In addition to being a preeminent researcher, Professor Joskow has trained a generation of scholars at MIT who now teach around the globe. He also works closely with industry, government, and nongovernmental organizations. He is a director of the Exelon Corporation and the TransCanada Corporation, a trustee of Yale

University, and a member of the Board of Overseers of the Boston Symphony Orchestra. He previously served as a director of the New England Electric System, National Grid, plc, State Farm Indemnity Company, and Whitehead Institute of Biomedical Research. Professor Joskow has been a member of the EPA's Acid Rain Advisory Committee and has served on the Environmental Economics Committee of the EPA's Science Advisory Board.

In this monograph, Professor Joskow reviews what is known and—equally important—what is not known about deregulation. As the world economy muddles through a financial crisis with few modern parallels, reregulation seems the order of the day. Some added government oversight is undoubtedly justified. But without careful, well-informed design, the consequences will surely be problematic. Professor Joskow provides the point of departure for this analysis, suggesting a research agenda for economists and others seeking to understand when new regulatory institutions are likely to be socially beneficial and how they should be designed.

Like all publications of the AEI Center for Regulatory and Market Studies, this monograph can be downloaded at no cost from www.reg-markets.org. We encourage educators to use and distribute these materials to their students.

ROBERT W. HAHN, Executive Director
AEI Center for Regulatory and Market Studies

Deregulation:
Where Do We Go from Here?

Paul L. Joskow

Over the past thirty years, the United States and many other countries have experienced a revolution in the extent and nature of the mechanisms used by government to regulate the structure, behavior, and performance of many markets for goods and services (Winston 1993, 2006; Peltzman and Winston 2000; Joskow 2005). This era of reform is often referred to as the era of "deregulation." The word *deregulation*, however, is a simplistic characterization of a much more complex process that involves the relaxation of government controls over prices and entry, the restructuring of industry to facilitate competition in some industry segments and better regulation in others, stricter but more effective environmental regulation, and efforts to improve the performance of product quality and safety and workplace safety regulations to increase the net benefits to society. Many of these reforms have been beneficial to our economy, and ongoing reforms have the promise of further enhancing economic performance.

Where Regulatory Reform Stands Today

The generally favorable assessments of regulatory reform over the past thirty years, however, have been tainted by the financial market crisis and its adverse effects on the real economy. We have what seems to be an ever-growing list of explanations for the causes of the financial market mess, with an even longer list of proposed regulatory, institutional, and governance reform initiatives to mitigate the problems in the short run and keep them from recurring in the long run. The present crisis was clearly caused by a combination of public policy failures reinforced by behavioral failures of private sector financial institutions, intermediaries, rating agencies, creditors, borrowers, and regulators. My own view, however, is that we still do not yet fully understand these public policy and private sector failures and the interactions between them that caused the problems. We necessarily know even less about the appropriate long-run public policy and private sector institutional reforms to keep these problems from emerging again. As with the Great Depression, scholars will be studying this period for many years. Similarly, if history is any guide, the rush to implement reforms in response to the immediate crisis without fully understanding its causes and developing comprehensive measures to address the market failures is likely to lead to at least some "quick and dirty" regulatory initiatives that fail to solve the problems and may even make them worse. This reaction is especially problematic in the case of regulating financial products, financial institutions, and financial markets because our understanding of the causes of systemic risk are relatively undeveloped, and many of the relevant markets are global.

Ironically, one of the few important sectors of the economy not subject to comprehensive regulatory reform during the past thirty years has been the financial services sector and the associated financial products and financial markets where such products are traded. Yet financial institutions, financial instruments, the markets where these products are traded, and the geographical expanse of trading have all changed dramatically over that period. While it has become routine to place a large share of the blame for the current financial crisis on deregulation, the list of federal and state regulatory agencies with jurisdiction over banks, insurance companies, brokerage firms, mutual funds, hedge funds, other financial institutions, and the products and markets where they trade, is as long as my left arm. The one thing we can be sure of is that we have no shortage of regulatory agencies with overlapping responsibilities for investor protection, financial market behavior and performance, and systemic risk mitigation that collectively were supposed to work to keep this kind of financial market mess from occurring. These regulatory agencies have overlapping jurisdictions, opaque goals, arbitrarily limited authorities, and histories that can often be traced back to Great Depression–era financial markets and economic conditions. These regulatory institutions have evolved over the past seventy-five years in a haphazard fashion that has not responded effectively to the evolution of financial institutions, products, and markets, but more as a series of fingers in the dike to try to keep new leaks from damaging the integrity of the entire dam.

Some regulatory changes that might be properly characterized as "deregulation"—such as the 1999 repeal of the provision of the Glass-Steagall Act of 1933 that prohibited bank holding companies from providing other types of financial services, the decision of the Securities and Exchange Commission (SEC) to end the uptick rule for short sales, and decisions to allow "sophisticated investors" to fend for themselves—have been idiosyncratic and not components of systematic regulatory institution reform. The reforms have sometimes been arbitrary (and initially cautious, such as the repeal of Regulation Q in 1980) and increasingly driven more by ideology than by the kind of comprehensive framework for regulatory reform in other industry contexts that has now become widely accepted by microeconomists..

Responsibility for the Financial Crisis. I think that history will reveal plenty of blame to go around for the current financial mess, implicating diverse interest groups, legislators, regulators, and the administrations that appointed them. In hindsight, the causes will encompass ideological perspectives from the left to the right. Blaming these problems simplistically on deregulation of financial instruments, financial markets, and financial institutions will not prove a useful framework for identifying good public policy reforms in this area. Accordingly, the policy problems that contributed to the current crisis are more properly conceptualized as a failure to engage in comprehensive reform of the entire regulatory framework governing financial institutions, products, and markets to better match the development of new financial instruments, trading platforms, market participants, and the globalization of financial markets. Some new regulations intended to control financial risk (for example, bank capital requirements under Basel II) may actually have contributed to the financial crisis by creating incentives to devise financial instruments (credit default swaps, for example) that appeared to turn certain risky assets into safe tier I capital. Poorly designed regulatory instruments can make a potentially bad situation worse.

But my focus here is not primarily on the financial market crisis and the appropriate policies to stop the bleeding and respond to lessons learned with public and private regulatory and institutional reforms. Rather, I am concerned that the ongoing efforts to understand and resolve this crisis—and what appears to be a widely accepted view that it can be blamed generically on "deregulation" and a "free market" mentality—will become a platform for launching a "reregulation" process in many other sectors of the economy that were deregulated over the past three decades. This *au courant* and undifferentiated trashing of deregulation more generally in the media has in turn provided a convenient opportunity for those self-interested in reregulating other industries and sectors or slowing down continuing regulatory reforms to blame deregulation for a long list of problems to feather their own nests rather than to promote the public interest.

Let me note as well that the modern deregulation, industry restructuring, and regulatory reform era did not start with George H. W. Bush, George W. Bush, or Ronald Reagan. If one must date it, the market liberalization and regulatory reform era started with Jimmy Carter and has been pursued by centrist Democrats and Republicans since then. Many of the deregulation, market liberalization, and market-friendly regulatory reforms of the past thirty years in the United States and many other countries have yielded significant benefits for their citizens and their economies. While these reforms have certainly not been perfect, reversing most of them would be harmful to our economy in the aggregate, although some interest groups might benefit.

A Critical Crossroads. I fear that we may be at a crossroads where we are moving from too much unprincipled relaxation of regulatory oversight in a few sectors to too much unprincipled and poorly designed reregulation in many others. And I attribute part of the blame for this unfortunate situation to the increasingly mindless debates about the role of government in the economy based on ideology rather than on clear goals and careful theoretical and empirical analysis of both market imperfections and regulatory imperfections. This trend has been reinforced by the increasing ideological polarization of so-called think tanks and their growing dependence on financial support from special interest groups. Of course, the American Enterprise Institute's Center for Regulatory and Market Studies has, from the beginning, stood for just the opposite—objective analysis of important regulatory issues based on clearly articulated goals, careful theoretical and empirical analysis, respect for principled differences of opinion, and willingness to change one's mind based on evidence. This is why I have been proud to have been associated with this center from the beginning.

In this monograph, I will make and support several points. First, I take as a given that even imperfectly competitive markets are extremely powerful institutions for allocating scarce resources efficiently, both statically and dynamically. Thus, while few markets satisfy the structural, behavioral, or performance assumptions of a textbook version of a perfectly competitive market, they are typically better than the next best alternative.

Second, we have a sound intellectual framework for evaluating when it makes sense to impose some form of government regulation on a particular market for goods and services, including regulation of financial institutions, financial products, and financial markets. The framework requires a good theoretical and empirical understanding of market *and* regulatory imperfections and the costs of each. The issues here are not properly characterized as "regulation" versus "deregulation," but rather involve the application of a disciplined framework for identifying *whether*, *where*, and *how* government regulatory policies can, on balance, improve market performance, taking the costs of market imperfections, the benefits of regulatory constraints, and the costs of regulatory imperfections into account. The regulation-versus-deregulation mantra reflects an ideological debate, not a serious framework for evaluating the performance of real markets and real regulatory institutions. The proper framework for considering these issues is familiar to serious microeconomists who have studied regulation, deregulation, and regulatory reforms of various kinds over the past thirty years.

Third, these frameworks can and should be applied to financial institutions, products, and markets, taking into account their specific market and institutional attributes and any associated market imperfections. Financial markets do have special attributes, and their performance has broad implications for the performance of the rest of the economy. Accordingly, reasoning by analogy to ordinary markets for goods and services (for example, surface freight transportation) to develop and apply a good regulatory and institutional framework for financial institutions, financial instruments, and financial markets can be very dangerous.

Fourth, over the past three decades, deregulation, privatization, and regulatory reform initiatives—or the European term that I prefer, *market liberalization* initiatives— have generally benefited the economy and consumers in the United States and other countries. These bene-fits include lower costs, enhanced rates of product and process inno-vation, better matches between consumer preferences and product quality and safety, and more efficient price structures (not always lower prices, as some of the worst regulatory programs kept prices too low and caused shortages). These market liberalization and regulatory reform initiatives—for example, the privatization, restructuring, and regulatory reform policies applied to the British railroad system— have not always been successful, in the sense that they created more problems than they solved, and there is as much to learn from failed market liberalization efforts as from successful efforts.

Future regulatory reforms should be based on objective analysis of the costs of market imperfections, the benefits of alternative regulatory constraints aimed at mitigating these imperfections, and the (direct, but more importantly, indirect) costs of alternative regulatory mechanisms, recognizing that both the costs and the benefits are uncertain. Broad-brush ideological calls for reregulation or deregulation are dangerous. The fundamental question we should be seeking to answer is: *What is the best we can do in an imperfect world?*

Fifth, whatever conclusions one reaches about the need for and nature of regulation, deregulation, or regulatory reforms, those conclusions should be specific to the attributes of particular industries, products, firms, and consumer decisions and subject to periodic reevaluation as such attributes change and new information emerges about the performance of public and private institutions.

Government Regulation Defined

In thinking about deregulation, we should start by defining what *regulation* means. No markets in modern, developed economies are completely unregulated by government-created institutions in any meaningful sense. Markets in all modern, developed market economies operate within a basic set of governance institutions or what Williamson has called the basic institutions of capitalism (Williamson 1985). In the United States, these include common-law institutions like property rights, liability rules, and contracts, and the institutions for enforcing them. There are also basic firm and market institutions created by statute, such as those created by corporate law, including the framework for creating limited liability corporations, antitrust laws, bankruptcy laws, employment laws, environmental laws, and the like. While we can discuss the pros and cons or the details of alternative structures for these basic institutions of capitalism and how they are implemented and enforced, all twenty-first-century developed-market economies have them. Spending a lot of time talking about doing away with them completely is not constructive.

Thus, when we discuss regulation, deregulation, regulatory reform, or market liberalization, we are talking about it within a basic set of legal institutions that are generally accepted as providing a "minimal" framework for markets to work well. What is it, then, that we are "regulating," "deregulating," or "liberalizing"?

Price and Market Entry. Scholarly analysis of government regulation focused for many years on government regulation of price levels, price structures, and entry into markets for particular goods and services (Kahn 1970; Joskow 2007). These government regulatory actions are not included in the list of basic institutions of capitalism. Going back to the late nineteenth century, we can construct a long list of goods and services that have been subject to price or entry regulation: oil, natural gas production, oil and natural gas pipeline transportation, telecommunications services, surface freight transportation, electricity supplies, interest rates, bus and streetcar services, water and sewer services, taxi prices, milk prices, residential rents, and so forth. While some of these price and entry regulations were justified as necessary responses to the "natural monopoly problem" (Joskow 2007), one does not have to be much of a free market advocate to find the natural monopoly argument for many of these goods and services implausible. Clearly, something else was going on there beyond protecting consumers from monopoly prices and inefficient duplication of network facilities. And what typically does go on is the consequence of powerful interest groups using the power of government to benefit themselves at the expense of others (Stigler 1971) and to hide the associated "taxation by regulation" in a complex and nontransparent regulatory process (Posner 1971).

Quality and Safety Issues. Another dimension of government regulation has focused on product and service quality and safety and on workplace safety. These regulations include information disclosure rules, licensing and certification procedures, quality standards, and the like. At the federal level, these regulations are implemented by a long list of regulatory agencies like the Federal Trade Commission, the Occupational Safety and Health Administration, the National Highway Transportation Safety Commission, the Consumer Products Safety Commission, and the Food and Drug Administration, among many others. The regulations these agencies issue are typically also subject to a "gatekeeper" at the Office of Management and Budget called the Office of Information and Regulatory Policy, which is supposed to review the benefits and costs of regulations proposed by executive branch agencies. Indeed, much of the criticism of deregulation really concerns how regulatory responsibilities are enforced and how costs and benefits are calculated and balanced. The economists' rationale for regulation in these areas turns on market imperfections associated with the provision and effective use of information necessary to make wise decisions. As noted, in most of these cases the scholarly discussion centers less on whether there should be some type of regulation and more on identifying regulatory mechanisms that help consumers and businesses balance costs and benefits of various levels of product quality and safety in risky environments with imperfect and asymmetric information.

Environmental Regulation. A third important area of government regulation is the environment. Most of what we talk about in this area, at least at the federal level, has evolved over the past forty years. The federal government now regulates or can regulate, directly or indirectly, emissions of virtually everything that goes into the air, water, and ground. Here, again, the primary questions of interest have not been so much whether some type of regulation makes sense but rather what the most effective regulatory mechanism is and how stringent the regulations should be. Answering the latter question in turn requires evaluations of regulatory costs and benefits, and these are both uncertain and controversial.

Investor Protections and Prudential Regulation. A fourth (or fourth and fifth) area of regulation of contemporary relevance involves regulatory requirements of various kinds placed on corporations, financial intermediaries, financial products, and the financial markets where they are traded. It is useful to divide these regulations into those motivated (arguably) by "investor protection" goals and those motivated by "prudential" regulation goals, although the two cannot be separated completely. The Securities and Exchange Commission, the Commodities Futures Trading Commission, and the Financial Industry Regulatory Authority (formed in July 2007) fall in the category of investor protection, and the Federal Reserve Board and the Federal Deposit Insurance Corporation fall in the category of prudential regulation.

The responsibilities of the investor protection agencies, or at least the impacts of their efforts to fulfill their responsibilities, overlap as they affect the structure, behavior, and performance of financial products, financial intermediaries, the markets in which these products are traded, and the information available to investors about both the products and the counterparties they deal with. Many of the regulatory agencies and regulations can be traced back to the Great Depression and reflect rationales similar to those behind product quality and safety and workplace safety regulations. These regulations include financial disclosure rules, accounting rules, corporate governance rules, securities registration requirements, and the certification of securities ratings agencies.

The rationale here is the view that without good information about the financial attributes of firms that issue securities to the public, associated accounting standards, appropriate financial products, and rules governing the behavior of financial markets and who can participate in them, investors will be unable to make wise investment decisions. As these regulations have evolved, they have also reflected a view that the "little guys" need more help than the "big guys," who are supposedly better able to obtain and process the information necessary to make wise investment decisions. (The current financial crisis raises questions about this assumption.) In reality, financial services firms have also exercised their political power to exert influence over how these regulatory institutions have evolved to protect themselves, either from competition or from regulations they find objectionable.

Prudential regulation of banks and other financial institutions has been introduced to dampen macroeconomic shocks caused by whatever they are caused by, including systemic credit market dysfunctions. Prudential regulation flows from the view that unregulated markets for financial services will not adequately control bubbles, bank runs, systemic risks, financial market collapses, and the adverse effects of dysfunctional credit markets on the real economy. I must point out how the development, analysis, and implementation of regulation in this area have been relegated to the field of macroeconomics and, to a lesser extent, to finance economists, including international finance economists. It is striking how little of the learning about economic regulation and quality and safety regulation that has emerged over the past forty years based on research by *microeconomists* has crossed the bridge into *macrofinance*-land. The market-imperfections-versus-regulatory-imperfections framework for examining the case for regulation and the choice of regulatory instruments that I discuss below have barely seeped into the area of prudential regulation.

While I have classified the SEC as, arguably, an investor protection regulatory agency, its actions can have implications for prudential regulatory issues, as well. Its decisions may affect the kinds or magnitude of macroeconomic dislocations that drive prudential regulation. Its decisions also affect the information available to investors and some aspects of the behavior of corporations, financial intermediaries, and financial markets. It is not clear, however, that the SEC—staffed heavily by lawyers and accountants and historically focused on accounting standards, disclosure standards, and legal enforcement actions—had the capability to evaluate properly the wider impacts of some of its regulatory actions (for example, the decision to end the uptick rule for short selling in July 2007, the focus on unsophisticated investors, and the predominance of an enforcement mentality over a monitoring and analytical perspective). This is simply one example of the failure of the United States to develop an appropriate comprehensive regulatory framework for the financial sector with clear goals, responsibilities, and appropriate authorities.

Market Imperfections versus Regulatory Imperfections

How do we make an intellectually respectable case for implementing various types of government regulation, for removing them, or for changing the way we regulate? Competitive markets are a powerful mechanism for allocating scarce resources efficiently. In a sense, competitive markets combined with the basic legal institutions of modern developed-market economies represent the null hypothesis against which the case for additional regulation must be tested. The case for government regulatory interventions must start, but not stop, with the identification *and* quantification of one or more market imperfections (Winston 2006). It is impossible to regulate intelligently, even under the best of circumstances, without a clear articulation of the nature of the market imperfections whose costs we are trying to ameliorate.

Market Imperfections. Most markets are characterized by some type of imperfection. Few, if any, perfectly satisfy the assumptions underlying textbook models of perfect competition or the performance associated with the textbook models of perfect competition. But the social costs of these market imperfections vary widely from the trivial to the very large. The fact that one can identify one or more market imperfections does not make a case for imposing government regulations on the relevant market unless one believes in the existence of the benevolent, perfectly informed regulator whom we all know well from economic theory. If the benevolent, perfectly informed government regulator existed in reality, we would regulate every market. He does not exist.

Thus, we must look at the other side of the equation. What are the imperfections and costs of government regulatory mechanisms and institutions? When the benefits of reducing the costs of market imperfections are compared to the costs of regulation, are we, on balance, better off? Regulation carries with it its own costs—direct implementation costs—but, more important, it carries indirect costs that can make market performance worse than it was when we simply accepted imperfect markets without trying to improve performance by regulating them. One of the worst mistakes made by policymakers is to assume that government regulatory institutions pursue some well-defined public interest, are well informed, can easily and without cost mitigate the market imperfections identified, and are not influenced by interest group politics.

The decision to regulate and the decision to change regulatory policies—whether to eliminate a set of regulatory constraints or change the form of those constraints—must rest on a careful balancing of the likely costs of market imperfections and the likely costs of alternative forms of regulation designed to mitigate them (imperfectly). This assessment should be dynamic, recognizing that technological change will affect consumer, firm, product, process, and industry attributes and, in turn, that regulation can affect the rate and direction of the changes in these attributes, often negatively, but sometimes positively.

The right approach to thinking about regulation and deregulation was articulated very clearly by my undergraduate adviser, Alfred Kahn, who asks, what is the best that we can do in an imperfect world (Kahn 1979)?

A fairly standard list of market imperfections may lead to a case for some form of enhanced government regulatory intervention:

- *Market power*, with so-called natural monopoly being an extreme case (Joskow 2007). The political case for regulation here is probably stronger than the "welfare economics" case, because voters are not indifferent to the apparent first-order distributional consequences of higher prices charged by monopolies. That is, the "rectangles" related to the distribution impacts of monopoly pricing are much more important politically than are the Harberger "triangles" that measure deadweight losses. Of course, the welfare analysis becomes more interesting when we recognize that a monopoly is likely to expend some of the monopoly rents on costly strategies to protect its monopoly position.

- *Externalities* arising from the positive and negative impacts of agents' behavior on others that are not fully reflected in their supply and consumption decisions. Environmental regulation is the standard case. Externality problems are ultimately "missing market" problems arising from the transactions costs of internalizing these positive and negative impacts through bilateral bargaining in the presence of basic common-law institutions of property rights, torts, and contracts (Coase 1960). I suspect, as well, that prudential regulation of banks and other financial intermediaries is motivated by externality issues related to the social costs of systemic collapses of financial markets, although it would be helpful to have a clear definition of systemic risk, what causes it, and what its costs are, to better inform the design of both investor protection and prudential regulation institutions.

- *Information costs*, information asymmetries, and consumer/investor decision-making imperfections, and bounded rationality and transaction costs generally (Williamson 1975).

- *Incomplete contracts* arising from bounded rationality and transactions costs (Williamson 1985; Joskow 1987).

- *Corporate governance* imperfections arising from the separation of ownership and control associated with large, modern public corporations.

Regulatory Imperfections. The imperfections and associated costs of government regulatory policies designed to mitigate these market imperfections must, however, be carefully articulated and measured, as well. These direct and indirect costs of government regulation must be part of any sensible cost-benefit analysis of regulation, deregulation, or regulatory reform. As I have already emphasized, the perfectly informed regulator that rigorously pursues a widely accepted articulation of the public interest does not exist in reality. Good and effective regulation that improves upon even imperfect market outcomes is difficult, indeed. This is a consequence of the realities of regulation in practice:

- Even if they have the right goals, regulators are necessarily imperfectly informed about the firm and consumer attributes—including attitudes toward risk—that are necessary, even in theory, to regulate well (Laffont and Tirole 1993; Joskow 2007). Indeed, regulators are typically more poorly informed than the firms they regulate and often less informed about the attributes of the consumers they may be seeking to protect, leading to the potential for regulation to lead to costly distortions in costs, product attributes, and the rate and direction of innovation (regulator-induced moral hazard).

• The regulatory process is characterized by bureaucratic costs, can take a long time to produce decisions, and is inherently conservative in its treatment of new product and process technologies and risk and new and better ways of regulating. Regulators also easily become protective of the traditional regulatory mechanisms that characterize the status quo and promote their own importance. This problem becomes greater as regulatory agencies age.

• The regulatory process is subject to interest-group capture, political influence, and tremendous pressure to engage in (hidden) taxation by regulation (Stigler 1971; Posner 1971; Noll 1989). The modern field of political economy based on rational actor models of political behavior did not start with studies of regulation accidentally. This phenomenon goes well beyond simplistic models of capture by regulated firms and reflects the fact that regulatory agencies have things they can do to help one interest group and harm others, naturally leading them to become targets of political competition. This phenomenon is exacerbated over time as young, "expert" regulatory agencies become dominated by commissioners and senior staff who have come up through the political process and are sensitive to the same political considerations as their sponsors in the executive and legislative branches. In my view, this problem has become more serious as "independent" regulatory agencies, once heavily populated by reasonably independent technocratic experts with clear goals, have increasingly come to be populated by commissioners and senior staff with narrower political goals—whether on the right or on the left.

A useful framework for evaluating proposals to regulate, deregulate, and change the way we regulate can be structured by asking and answering a set of simple questions, though providing precise answers to these questions may often be quite difficult. I will articulate the questions from the perspective of proposed new regulations, but a similar set of questions can be applied to deregulation and adoption of new regulatory mechanisms:

- Precisely what are the market imperfections that the proposed regulations are trying to fix, and what are the causes of these market imperfections?

- What are the social costs of these market imperfections, and who bears them?

- Exactly what will be regulated, and how?

- What alternative regulatory arrangements may be available to mitigate the market imperfections, and why is one likely to be better than the other?

- What information and authority will a regulator need to implement the proposed regulations effectively?

- How much will the costs of market imperfections be reduced if the proposed regulations are implemented successfully?

- What are the likely *direct* costs of implementing the regulatory framework?

- What potential *indirect* costs may be incurred by implementing the proposed regulations, given imperfect and asymmetric information on the part of regulators with good intentions?

- On balance, what will be the likely net benefits or the likely net costs of the proposed regulations in practice?

The Record of Regulatory Reform

With all the recent hysteria about the evils of "deregulation," one would think the market liberalization and regulatory reforms of the past three decades have imposed enormous costs on the economy. To the contrary, with a few exceptions, just the opposite has been the reality, and some of the most significant costs have resulted from too little deregulation, privatization, and regulatory reform (Peltzman and Winston 2000; Winston 1993; Joskow and Rose 1989; Joskow 2005).

Price and Entry Regulation. Let me start with so-called economic regulation. By that term, I refer to the various forms of price and entry regulation typically implemented by state and federal regulatory agencies and sometimes by municipalities. It is useful to think back to 1978 to recall in how many areas price regulation and companion restrictions on competitive entry existed in the United States at that time: crude oil and petroleum products; natural gas production, transportation and distribution; surface freight transportation by trucks, trains, and barges; commercial passenger and freight airline service; telecommunications services; electricity generation, transmission, and distribution; cable television services; residential rents; milk prices, as well as broader agricultural support policies to keep prices from falling; and interest rates on bank accounts, among others.

Almost every one of these industries, services, or products has been subject to dramatic changes in the regulatory framework that existed only thirty years ago: deregulation of prices and entry, better regulation of remaining regulated segments, and industry restructuring programs to promote competition and better regulation. Overall, the results have been very good from a broad economic welfare perspective (Winston 1993; Peltzman and Winston 2000; Joskow 2005). While some things might have been done better and the potential for further reform still exists in some sectors, I find it hard to imagine that any right-thinking person would want to reverse these changes and return to the heavily regulated era of 1978.

Of course, unanticipated consequences have been associated with some of these reforms, some good and some bad. Where there have been problems, they can generally be attributed to poor regulation of the key network segments that competitive markets depend on to operate efficiently and to regulations that inefficiently restrict the development of competition in the deregulated segments. To oversimplify, the United States probably had too little deregulation of prices and entry, too little supporting regulatory reform, and too little industry restructuring in the sectors that have experienced the most serious transition problems.

Has everyone been made better off? Of course not. The business traveler whose airfare was paid by his employer has not benefited from airline deregulation. The wheat shipper close to a main line who could get rail transportation service at below-cost regulated prices from a bankrupt railroad is not better off. The local television stations that once had to compete for viewers and advertisers with only a very small number of other local stations and now face competition from distant signals and new channels delivered over cable systems are not better off. High-sulfur eastern coal mines are worse off because they now face more intense competition from low-sulfur western coal, at least partly as a consequence of railroad deregulation.

Making everyone better off with regulatory reforms is not the right standard. If it were, we would never change anything. It tells us only why some groups favor regulation and others oppose it. But when the long-term benefits to consumers and producers, including the effects of product and process innovations, are added up, the economy overall is generally much better off as a consequence of deregulation of prices and entry and associated regulatory and institutional reforms in most of these sectors.

In economic regulation, it is convenient to consider two groups of industries: those that were or potentially were structurally competitive in all horizontal segments, where "competitors" were properly defined; and those that had both competitive horizontal segments and, at least initially, one or more horizontal network segments that had natural monopoly characteristics and would require some type of continuing regulation to allow competition to flourish in other horizontal segments.

In the first group, we have, for example, airlines; trucks, trains, and barges shipping freight, and oil and natural gas production (distinct from oil and gas transportation).These are the cleanest cases where simple deregulation of prices and entry made sense because there were many actual or potential competing firms and limited scale economies and barriers to competitive entry. The results of deregulation of prices and entry in these industries have generally been as anticipated: improvements in productivity, faster technological innovation, more efficient (not necessarily lower) prices, better-quality service, and increased investment to expand supply (Peltzman and Winston 2000; Rose 1987; Debande 1999; Belman and Monaco 2001; Hubbard 2003).

Airlines. People naturally raise questions about airline deregulation because it has not worked out exactly as anticipated. They seem to have fond memories of the quality of service provided under the old regulatory regime but forget how costly it was. Since 1978, airline productivity is higher, costs per seat-mile are lower, airfares are lower, load factors are much higher, and the quality of service is lower, though many fail to recall that one of the arguments for deregulation was that load factors, service quality, and the associated costs were too high under regulation (Morrison and Winston 2000). In 1978, I do not think anyone expected the extensive price discrimination (nonpejorative) that has been observed or a competitive equilibrium for airlines characterized by a smaller number of large national airlines rather than a much larger number of small airlines.

Today, we understand much better the attributes of imperfectly competitive markets with scale and network economies and diverse consumer preferences for quality than we did in 1978. While this better understanding might not have affected the normative case for deregulating prices and entry for airline service, it might have changed other policies that would have provided better infrastructure and institutional support for a competitive airline industry.

The most costly disappointments of price and entry deregulation in airlines can be traced to some other institutional factors. Air traffic has expanded dramatically over the past thirty years. Passenger enplanements have increased by about 180 percent. Departures (and presumably landings) have increased by about 125 percent. Yet airport capacity has hardly expanded at all, inevitably leading to more crowded airports and delays. Only one new major hub airport has been built since 1978 (Denver). It takes ten to fifteen years to build a new runway at a major airport. Three new runways were completed in 2008, after roughly twelve years of planning, regulatory reviews, and construction. Because the government has been reluctant to implement sensible policies to ration scarce airport capacity, we get queues and long delays. Our antiquated air traffic control system, owned and controlled by an agency of the federal government, undermines the efficient use of scarce airspace and further contributes to delays, especially when weather is poor. Other countries have commercialized their air traffic control systems with superior results (McDougall and Roberts 2009). We have a global commercial air transport industry, but the United States and most other countries place major barriers in the way of creating global air carriers that can compete worldwide with one another. In short, we have not created the supporting government-controlled and government-regulated network infrastructure that would be most desirable for supporting a competitive commercial air traffic market, and we have not fully opened up entry to potential competitors from other countries.

Finally, policymakers have not been aggressive enough in imposing and implementing regulations that require the airlines to be more transparent about what their responsibilities are when they enter into a contract with a customer—called a "confirmed airplane ticket." When I buy seat M16 at Symphony Hall in Boston for a Saturday night performance, I expect that my seat will be there when I arrive, and not a "sorry we are overbooked" sign. At least some of the trials and tribulations of air travel would be more tolerable if the terms and conditions of carriage were transparent and applied consistently. And the focus of reregulation has properly been on something like a flier's bill of rights, although general transparency requirements might be all that is needed.

In short, I do not believe that a good case can be made for reregulating the commercial airline industry, returning it to what it was in 1978. A good case can be made, though, for doing a better job with the necessary infrastructure for supporting competition and for requiring more articulation of consumers' rights associated with the tickets they purchase.

Railroads. Another case that raises questions in some quarters is the deregulation of railroad freight rates, entry, and exit and the extensive reorganization that has occurred among the railroads through merger and exit since 1980 (Grimm and Winston 2000). These mergers have generally led to lower costs (Bitzan and Wilson 2007). Transport rates for important classes of shippers have declined (Vachal et al. 2006). Some shippers argue that they are being overcharged by the railroads, in the sense that the railroads are charging more than the "competitive level," whatever that may be. Maybe that is true in some cases where rates have risen. Intramodal and intermodal competition faced by railroads is certainly not perfect competition. Moreover, given the economic characteristics of railroad costs, there are necessarily varying degrees of market power, in the textbook sense that prices for some services are greater than their short-run marginal costs. A price structure involving second- and third-degree price discrimination is, however, a necessary attribute of an industry with these attributes that must both satisfy a break-even constraint and do so efficiently.

Moreover, the earlier regulatory regime is not a model of good performance. It led virtually all U.S. railroads into bankruptcy, halted their incentive and ability to invest adequately in their networks and modern rolling stock, and stymied innovation, including more effective integration with truck transportation. These adverse consequences of regulation were enormously costly to our economy. Even after deregulation, railroads have not, overall, earned excessive rates of return. In addition, so-called captive shippers can still make their case for lower rates if they choose to do so, because the rates charged to so-called captive shippers continue to be subject to potential regulatory review. Indeed, two years ago, the Surface Freight Transportation Board, which is responsible for implementing these regulations, adopted new rules to reduce the cost and time of litigation associated with these residual railroad transportation rate regulations. The railroad industry, perhaps more than others, also encountered integration problems associated with the extensive merger and restructuring wave that occurred as the industry rationalized after regulatory restrictions on prices and consolidation were lifted. Perhaps the deregulation process could have anticipated those problems better, but I doubt it. Overall, railroad deregulation has been a big win for the U.S. economy and for the environment.

Let us turn now to the other group of industries subject to deregulation of prices and entry, restructuring requirements, and network regulatory reform. This group includes natural gas transportation and distribution, electric power, telecommunications, and cable TV. It would be wrong to characterize the reforms that have been introduced in these sectors over the past two or three decades as simply deregulation; this would be an oversimplification of a much more complex process of industry structure and regulatory reform that took place over many years. Calling it deregulation seriously understates the nature of the reform challenge and what has been accomplished as a result of these reforms.

While this is not the place to engage in a detailed discussion of all these industry cases, most of them share some common themes (cable TV being the major exception to the basic reform model). Under the old regulatory regime, each of these sectors was characterized by extensive vertical integration from the upstream production to the downstream delivery level, either through common ownership or very long-term regulated contractual arrangements. The entire chain of production was subject to price and entry regulation by either federal or state regulators, or sometimes both. The general argument for regulation was that a natural monopoly or oligopoly problem called for it to mitigate real or imagined market power.

During the 1970s and 1980s, however, there was a growing recognition that while some vertical segments of these industries (natural gas transportation, for example) might have natural monopoly characteristics that could indicate a need for continuing—perhaps better—price and entry regulation, other segments (for example, natural gas production, processing, marketing, and storage) were or could be quite competitive. For regulated industries with these characteristics, there has been a basic reform model

- to separate (structurally or functionally) the potentially competitive segments from the monopoly or oligopoly network segments that would be regulated;

- to remove price and entry regulation from the competitive segments;

- to unbundle the sale of regulated network service from competitive services;

- to establish transparent prices for access to and use of the network; and

- to allow end-users (local distribution companies or end-use consumers in the case of gas and electricity, and end-use consumers in the case of telecommunications) to choose their suppliers of competitive services and have them arrange to have that service "shipped" to them over an open-access network with a regulated cap on the prices for providing transportation service.

This is the basic regulatory reform model applied to most of these industries, though the devil is in the details, and the details vary from industry to industry. Moreover, as time passes, technology changes may undermine, and have in many cases undermined, the initial assumptions about where the "natural monopoly" segments begin and end. The prospect of product and process innovations requires, in theory, a regulatory framework that encourages innovations and can adapt quickly to them. This kind of dynamic regulatory framework, which has been difficult to design and put into practice, represents the greatest cost of continuing regulation of residual segments of these industries. Sunset provisions might provide just the kind of incentives regulators need to take such changes more seriously.

Natural Gas. The regulatory and structural reforms that have been applied to the natural gas industry are not widely publicized, understood, or even studied these days (MacAvoy is an exception; see MacAvoy 2000). This neglect is unfortunate, because the natural gas industry provides an excellent model for the successful implementation of regulatory and structural reforms in industries with these characteristics.

Some history here would be helpful. Municipalities and some states began regulating local gas distribution companies during the mid-1800s. Most of these local gas companies manufactured low-heating-value gas from coal for local distribution, primarily for use in lighting and cooking. As large deposits of *natural* gas were discovered, typically in conjunction with the exploration for and production of oil, and as long-distance, high-pressure pipeline technology advanced, interstate pipeline networks began to transport what was often "waste gas" from production regions to consuming areas. The early development of the natural gas industry was largely unregulated from a price and entry perspective.

The federal government (through the Federal Power Commission, which later became the Federal Energy Regulatory Commission) began to regulate the price of interstate pipeline service beginning in the late 1930s as part of the general expansion of federal regulation to public utilities and holding companies. Interstate activities were becoming much more important in the electricity, natural gas, and telecommunications industries as technological change fostered expansions in the geographic scope of trade beyond state boundaries. Federal regulation filled a perceived regulatory gap resulting from state regulation of these industries. At that time, interstate pipelines acquired gas through contract from independent or affiliated producers at unregulated market prices and resold it to local distributers and large customers under contract. Local distribution companies then resold the gas to end-use customers at state-regulated prices, passing through the costs they paid for gas they purchased from pipelines.

The natural gas industry expanded rapidly after the Second World War, and new pipelines brought growing volumes of gas from Louisiana, Oklahoma, and Texas to cities in the Midwest, Northeast, and other areas that had previously relied primarily on coal and oil for heating and boiler fuel. Natural gas was cleaner, more efficient, and more convenient to use than coal, oil, or manufactured gas; and where it was available, it became the fuel of choice in many end-use applications and in the generation of electricity in areas that did not have access to cheap coal.

The rapidly increasing demand for natural gas led to higher prices, as the commodity that had been essentially a waste product produced naturally in conjunction with oil gained significant value in its own right. Local gas distribution consumers and large end-use customers argued that federal regulation should be extended to the price of natural gas produced in the field to keep prices from rising and allowing gas producers to earn competitive market rents higher than they had ever dreamed. The economic reality was not a problem of seller market power, but rather the desire of buyers to use regulation to exercise monopsony power on their behalf. The legal reality was different. The Supreme Court agreed with the legal arguments that the Federal Power Commission had the statutory obligation to regulate the field price of natural gas in *Phillips Petroleum Co. v. Wisconsin* (347 U.S. 672) in 1954. As a result of this decision, the Federal Power Commission was then charged with regulating the field price of natural gas as well as the prices for transporting it through the interstate pipeline system. It embarked on this quest by trying to set cost-based regulated prices for natural gas produced by thousands of producers located in many different production basins. The Commission did not get very far before concluding that producer-by-producer regulation was not feasible because of the large number of producers and a lengthy cost-based regulatory process. It then adopted what it thought would be a less burdensome and more sensible approach by setting cost-based prices for all the gas produced in large production basins from reserves discovered in different time periods—that is, the Commission held "area rate proceedings" to establish regulated prices for gas discovered at different times in individual gas-producing areas. These area rate proceedings also took many years. The price of gas delivered by pipelines then involved the "rolling together" of the varying regulated prices determined through this process.

This regulatory scheme virtually ensured that prices paid by pipelines for gas produced in the gas fields would be too low to clear supply and demand, and by the 1970s, serious natural gas shortages emerged both in the form of rationing to existing gas customers and denying hookups to new gas customers requesting service. The primary problem was that the regulation of the field prices of natural gas kept these prices from rising sufficiently to balance supply and rapidly growing demand. The shortage problems got even worse as oil prices rose in 1974 and again in 1979–81 as consumers sought to switch from oil to low-priced gas whose price was constrained by regulation. Although natural gas was relatively cheap, many consumers could not get it at any price because of both price regulation and restrictions on resale of incumbent rights to regulated-price natural gas.

The primary beneficiaries of natural gas price regulation at that time were Canadian producers who could sell into the U.S. market at high unregulated prices and customers with legacy gas contracts who paid prices well below market-clearing levels. These contracts could not be resold and were slowly coming to an end.

The growing shortages of natural gas helped to stimulate a shift in policy toward deregulation of natural gas field prices. The Natural Gas Policy Act of 1978 began the long process of deregulating the field price of natural gas. This process accelerated during the 1980s, and by the early 1990s, price regulation of natural gas field was completely gone. During a long transition period, however, the same molecules of natural gas were being sold in the field at many different prices, depending on when gas supply contracts regulated by the Federal Energy Regulatory Commission (FERC) between producers and pipelines, between pipelines and distribution companies, and between pipelines and large industrial and electric utility customers were signed. These contracts were rolled together to give consumers a blended price that was *initially* lower than the prevailing market price for deregulated new natural gas supplies available to clear the market. The shortages continued.

Then, in the mid-1980s, the unregulated market price for new natural gas fell dramatically, and for many years it stayed at much lower levels than those that had prevailed during the early 1980s. Meanwhile, regulated contract prices were now often *higher* than unregulated market prices. Local gas distribution companies and large direct pipeline service customers argued that FERC should reset the contract prices to reflect lower natural gas prices or, instead, that pipeline customers should be permitted to reject these contracts, buy gas directly from producers, and arrange separately to have the gas shipped to them over the same pipelines using unbundled, FERC-regulated pipeline transportation charges. The producers with the high-priced contracts and the pipelines with the obligations to take and pay for gas under these contracts were not impressed with the case for market-based pricing.

And so began a long process through which FERC unwound the web of contracts based on decades of price regulation linking producers, pipelines, and distribution contracts; unbundled transportation service from the production and marketing of natural gas; reformed the regulation of pipeline transport rates by setting generous price caps; and encouraged negotiated transportation contracts. The states also began to require that local distribution companies use transparent competitive bidding programs to acquire gas supplies separately from pipeline services. Some states followed by unbundling local distribution service for smaller retail customers, as well.

The mixture of deregulation, industry restructuring, and light-handed regulation of pipeline transportation and storage has been very successful and has delivered benefits to producers, pipelines, and consumers:

- A reasonably well-integrated North American market for natural gas supplies (Cuddington and Wang 2006);

- A large integrated North American pipeline system that has grown and adapted to changing supply and demand conditions;

- A more efficient end-use pricing system in which delivered gas prices are now more closely aligned with changes in supply and demand conditions for natural gas (whose price has varied by a factor of four in the past year alone);

- Growing competition in the pipeline sector as investors are free to seek to build new pipeline capacity to service new gas supply regions with few regulatory hurdles, as they are doing even now to provide the transportation service for the growing supplies of natural gas in the Rockies and from shale gas deposits in Texas, Louisiana, and Canada, which will reduce pipeline congestion and better integrate the Far West market with the rest of Canada and the United States;

- Innovation in gas exploration and production techniques, dramatically increasing North American gas supplies above what was expected only a few years ago, as well as innovations in pipeline construction and operations and natural gas storage.

Electric Power. With respect to the deregulation, industry restructuring, and network regulatory reform of electric power sectors, I have written enough that my views are well known (Joskow 2000, 2006, 2008). Accordingly, I will be brief. The electric power industry can be restructured and its regulation reformed by applying a model similar to the successful model provided by the natural gas industry, adapted to reflect the special physical attributes of electricity. This type of reform program, adopted in England and

Wales in the 1990s, works very well. It began to be adopted in the United States in the late 1990s but was slowed down considerably after the California electricity crisis in 2001. We now have some parts of the country with fully liberalized electricity systems (New York, most of New England, and Texas), those with the more or less traditional system of a regulated, vertically integrated monopoly, and those somewhere in between.

This bizarre mixture of competition and regulation for suppliers using the same physical electric power network is inefficient and establishes a poor platform for proposed new energy and environmental policy initiatives targeted at the electric power sector. The problems here are not technical or economic. They are political, as incumbents resist restructuring, deregulation, and regulatory reform; as states seek to protect their regulatory prerogatives; and as a consequence of eight years with a presidential administration that gave little if any support for this kind of deregulation program in the electric power sector, despite the fact that Texas has perhaps the most complete and successful electricity liberalization program in the country. President George W. Bush brought an outstanding individual from Texas to lead FERC's deregulation program—a program that had advanced significantly during the Clinton administration—but did not energetically support his efforts. The one thing the Bush administration cannot be accused of is aggressive support for deregulation in the electric power sector.

Telecommunications. The process of introducing competition into telecommunications, an industry that was a virtually complete end-to-end regulated monopoly controlled by AT&T and its subsidiaries (including a monopoly over customer premises equipment and network switching equipment) from the 1920s until regulatory reforms gained speed in the 1970s, has been long and tedious (Crandall 1991). The conventional wisdom prior to the 1970s was that the old system worked well and was quite innovative. I will not repeat the telecommunications restructuring, deregulation, and regulatory reform story here since, unlike the natural gas story, it is well documented in the literature (Crandall 1991; Joskow and Noll

1999; Crandall and Hausman 2000). There are, however, some lessons to be learned.

First, the original reform model, and the model upon which the antitrust cases against AT&T and policies of the Federal Communications Commission (FCC) to encourage competition were based, assumed that the local network was a natural monopoly, and that promoting competition in other segments of the industry required extensive regulation of the terms and conditions of access to the local network (Joskow and Noll 1999). Designing the terms and conditions of access to the local network was relatively straightforward when it focused on giving consumers access to competing suppliers of intercity service, though it required unwinding a complicated web of cross-subsidies from intercity service to local service and from urban consumers to rural consumers. In the end, reform was easier in theory than in practice, especially during the period when AT&T had to compete with other suppliers of intercity service at the same time it had to provide them with access to its local networks at regulated prices. The transition was messy but necessary until competing intercity networks could expand.

The challenge of designing policies to promote competition at the local network level was more significant and more complicated and was plagued by more missteps (Crandall and Hausman 2000; Hausman 1999; Vogelsang 2003). At the very least, we must admit that regulating the prices, terms, and conditions of access to individual unbundled local network elements was both technically challenging and poorly implemented. Indeed, the whole idea that encouraging competitors to "compete" at the local network level largely by buying and reselling all the elements of the incumbent's network would result in social benefits is questionable, unless it were part of a rapid transition to real facility-based competition. Getting the prices of local network elements right was almost impossible, and the disincentives to investment resulting from getting the prices wrong were potentially very costly, discouraging innovation (Hausman 1997). At worst, the entire exercise was doomed to failure.

Second, in fact, competition to provide local service by and large came from real facility-based innovations that were largely unanticipated when the original reform model was conceived, rather than through the implementation of unbundled network elements access pricing policies applied to incumbent network owners (Swann and Loomis 2005). The primary competition for local service now comes from cable companies and from wireless service. The program for unbundling network elements led to few technological improvements in the local networks and may have retarded such innovation. In particular, it probably slowed down investments in local networks that would have enabled the local telephone companies to compete effectively with cable companies to provide high-speed broadband service and video services sooner than has been the case.

The lesson here is that any regulatory reform program must anticipate that transforming innovations may occur on the supply and demand sides and should be structured to adapt quickly. The difficulty of designing regulatory processes with these attributes must be considered one of the potential dynamic costs of regulation. Regulatory mechanisms that restrict the development and diffusion of new and better products and services can be very costly. Facilitating technological innovations that reduce costs or bring new and better products to market convey "first-order" efficiency benefits to the economy ("rectangles" in cost-benefit space), while static monopoly problems per se are "second-order" efficiency losses ("triangles" in cost-benefit space).

Cable Television. I will conclude this section with a few observations about the regulation of cable television (Crawford 2000; U.S. Federal Communications Commission 2000). This industry was started as an unregulated industry by entrepreneurs who sought to bring television service to rural areas where it was unavailable. For example, I am told that cable TV was brought to Ithaca, New York, by the owner of a local appliance store who wanted to sell television sets to the people who lived there but who could not get direct over-the-air TV reception. Because the cable companies had to cross public rights-of-way and use poles owned by the telephone or electric companies, they needed a municipal franchise. The pole attachments rights from these other utilities were in turn regulated by state public utility commissions, and the early municipal franchises were non-exclusive. Initially, the interest of cable TV investors in large urban areas, where there were typically three or more local stations, was quite limited because the cable companies had little to offer except to rebroadcast the signals of TV stations which potential subscribers could already receive free over the air.

As local cable systems expanded in remote areas and the local populations bought television sets, concerns began to be raised about cable service prices. At the same time, cable operators making substantial investments in new facilities were interested in having their franchises become exclusive. Thus began to emerge a mutually beneficial local franchising process where municipalities gave cable operators exclusive franchises, sometimes through competitive bidding, in return for price guarantees, price adjustment procedures, and other benefits for the municipalities (for example, wiring government buildings without charge and offering a special municipal channel).

Technology marched on. Cable operators discovered that they could import more distant signals by using microwave technology, expand the quality of service, increase demand for cable service, and raise prices. Cable operators then discovered that they could offer additional services—movies—for a separate fee. The innovation adopted by HBO to deliver its movie and sports service via satellite to cable systems that installed the necessary reception equipment greatly reduced the costs and expanded the diffusion of "premium" movie services. Ted Turner soon followed by putting his local independent broadcast station in Atlanta (WTBS) on the satellite as well, charging a fee to cable operators for retransmitting it. The additional programming made cable service of greater interest to viewers in cities that had multiple free over-the-air broadcast services, and new cable systems began to spread to more and more cities where the population had access to multiple free over-the-air stations.

The use of microwave and satellite transmission and the rebroadcast of signals from broadcast stations brought the federal government into the act. And eventually, the FCC (prodded by Congress) decided that the emerging new technology both had (real or imagined) natural monopoly characteristics and threatened the economic models of local "free" broadcast stations by creating more competition. While this competition was good for consumers, it was not good for the local stations that were well represented in Washington and used their political influence to thwart the rapid growth of competition from cable systems. Hence, the FCC began to regulate the services that cable operators were permitted to offer and eventually was charged with regulating cable service prices.

In the meantime, new cable-only channels emerged as the technology for distributing many more channels on cable networks advanced, and the number of subscribers to cable service increased as well. These new services were attractive to consumers, increased the demand for cable service, and further threatened the broadcast networks and local stations. Prices for cable service rose as the quality of services, demand, and delivery costs increased. Broadcast networks and local stations faced even more intense competition. In 1984, Congress stepped in, passing the Cable Television Policy Act to impose a broad set of regulatory restrictions on subscriber prices, ownership arrangements, franchise provisions and renewals, channel usage, and the like, with the goal of reducing the rate of increase in subscriber prices and promoting competition. Subscriber prices continued to increase rapidly, however, and the hoped-for competition did not emerge.

Congress next passed the 1992 Cable Television Consumer Protection and Competition Act, which further tightened FCC regulation of cable TV prices (Crawford 2000). The expectation was that the new regulatory framework would lead to a 10 percent drop in the average subscriber price. Instead, the average cable bill rose. The FCC imposed a further reduction in per-channel charges in 1994 with limited impact and then began to bring the ineffective regulation to an end. In 1996, the Telecommunications Policy Act phased out subscriber rate regulation under the assumption that competition from telephone companies and wireless providers would emerge to constrain the market power of incumbent television companies. During this entire period, cable system capacity grew rapidly, along with the number of programs available to subscribers. The share of households subscribing to cable television continued to increase. Facility-based competition from local telephone companies and wireless technologies emerged more slowly than expected, but provisions in the 1996 act that reduced barriers to entry ultimately helped stimulate it. In this way a bizarre cycle of regulation, deregulation, reregulation, and deregulation came to an end.

There are a number of lessons here as well:

- Regulating in the context of rapidly expanding numbers and qualities of services offered by suppliers is very difficult and often counterproductive;

- Incumbents will spend large amounts of money to retard competition;

- Even imperfect competition is likely to yield results superior to price and entry regulation;

- The most important regulatory innovations are those that promote competition rather than those that seek to control real or imagined market-power problems.

Environmental Regulation. Few economists would disagree that environmental externality problems create a good case for government regulation of emissions into the air, water, and land that are harmful to the health or well-being of individuals or that increase costs for businesses that must cope with them. I realize some believe that the solutions to such problems can all be left to common-law enforcement of property rights and use of liability rules, but I think that is a fringe view.

The primary economic controversies regarding environmental regulations turn on questions of what emissions should be regulated (is the likely harm greater than the direct and indirect costs of regulation?), how stringently emissions should be controlled (what level of emissions balances the environmental harm and the costs of mitigation?), what mechanisms should be used to regulate (source-specific standards; prices, that is, emissions taxes; quantities, that is, cap and trade, hybrid systems, and the like?); and how the rules should be enforced. The legitimate differences of opinion on these questions can lead to a lot of controversy. Characterizing such controversies as regulation versus deregulation, however, rarely makes much sense, although there are certainly important cases such as greenhouse gases (GHG) and mercury in which the regulation-versus–no-regulation bridge must be crossed first.

The first two questions—what emissions should be regulated and how stringently they should be controlled—are necessarily difficult to answer with precision because the measurement of environmental harm and mitigation costs is necessarily uncertain and subject to change over time. Most economists, though, believe we should at least try to perform the best cost-benefit analysis we can, given the information available, and leave room for policy adaptation as more information is obtained. We must recognize, however, that there is much disagreement over how these cost-benefit analyses can best be done and the values that should be placed on key variables (for example, value of a human life, morbidity costs, recreational values, nonuse values, revealed preferences versus contingent valuation methods, and so forth). Exemplifying such disagreements are the controversies among distinguished economists about the proper discount rate and utility function parameters to use for evaluating the trajectory of constraints on GHG emissions (Nordhaus 2007; Weitzman 2007; Stern 2007). As time passes, new scientific and epidemiological evidence may lead to higher or lower estimates of the damages than originally thought. We also know from experience that, with the right incentives, the costs of mitigation have often turned out to be lower than was originally thought as innovative emissions control technologies are identified and used.

The one area of substantial agreement among economists is with regard to the best *mechanisms* for controlling emissions, given targets for how tight the constraints should be. The regulatory mechanisms historically favored by environmental regulators have been source-specific emissions or technology standards. These regulatory approaches, though, fail to recognize that the cost of reducing emissions varies widely depending on the source, that new and better emissions control technologies may be developed and deployed with the right incentives, that meeting aggregate emissions reduction targets using this approach depends heavily on assumptions about industry developments over time (the rate of growth in demand for the product or domestic production versus imports, for example), and that regulatory approaches have tended to be litigation-intensive, delaying achievement of environmental goals.

Instead, economists have come to favor the use of market-based mechanisms to control emissions where the implementation costs are not excessive: emissions charges, cap-and-trade systems, or hybrid systems that combine cap and trade with a backstop price for more emissions permits. These mechanisms all involve creating a price for emissions and then allowing those covered by the program to adapt to the prices in the most economical fashion available to them. There is a well-developed theoretical literature on the factors that favor price, quantity, or hybrid approaches (Weitzman 1974; Roberts and Spence 1992). The choice depends on the nature of the uncertainty about the benefits and costs of mitigation and the shapes of the benefit and cost functions. Despite the teachings of this literature, the choices among market-based approaches have in practice turned primarily on political considerations (Joskow and Schmalensee 1998). The public does not like direct taxes, and market-based approaches appear to be more easily adopted if they are formulated as cap-and-trade systems (perhaps with a backstop price).

We now have a lot of experience with cap-and-trade systems in the United States, drawn from programs for eliminating lead in gasoline and for controlling sulfur dioxide emissions and NOx emissions from power plants (Ellerman et al. 2000). We are also gaining experience with the application of a cap-and-trade system to control emissions of CO_2 in Europe (Joskow and Ellerman 2008). These systems work well in reducing costs, encouraging diverse and innovative mitigation responses, and meeting environmental goals on schedule. They are also well adapted to new information about the relevant costs and benefits, since the government can buy allowances and retire them to tighten constraints or increase the supply of allowances to reduce the constraints.

The notion that there has been deregulation of emissions into the air, water, and land is nonsense. Nor is it the case that the quality of the environment has generally deteriorated in the past several decades. At least for the traditional air emissions covered by the Clean Air Act (that is, excluding greenhouse gases), the record is clear that emissions have declined and air quality has improved over the past fifteen years, continuing a trend that goes back to 1970. And except for ground-level ozone, microparticulates and (now) mercury, virtually the entire population lives in areas that meet the national ambient air quality standards. Stratospheric ozone is recovering, and concentrations of ozone-depleting chemicals are declining. Reversing a long-term trend, wetland acreage increased in the past decade. Drinking water quality has improved. Hazardous-waste generation has declined significantly. Forest cover has increased in the United States. No doubt, environmental quality has deteriorated in some areas (such as the contamination of fish), though the Environmental Protection Agency has been particularly bad at developing useful environmental indicators and collecting the time series data accurately enough to measure relevant trends. Putting aside greenhouse gas emissions, however, the general trends are positive. Rather than deregulation, the real issues are whether the constraints on emissions are too tight or too lenient and whether we are meeting environmental goals as efficiently as possible.

The use of "deregulation" to characterize the last decade's policies affecting emissions that harm human health and welfare, then, must be a code word for something else. Perhaps "deregulation" refers to the Bush administration's failure to tighten further the national ambient air quality standards or to embrace a more aggressive greenhouse gas mitigation program, although it is hard to call this deregulation, since greenhouse gases were never regulated. Perhaps "deregulation" reflects a reaction to what is perceived as "stealth deregulation" through "lax" monitoring and enforcement and tighter cost-benefit standards applied by the Office of

Management and Budget. Stealth deregulation is wrong and is properly criticized if it involves a failure to enforce the law. The government should enforce the law faithfully and efficiently, whether it likes it or not, and go through administrative procedures and court reviews to seek legislative redress if it wants to change the way it implements the law. Different views on the relevant benefits and costs should be expected, however.

Most regulatory statutes give the executive branch and independent regulatory agencies substantial discretion in how they regulate and what they regulate, and the resources they devote to particular regulatory activities. Both Congress and the courts have oversight over these decisions and constrain that discretion. Nevertheless, different administrations have different views on a wide range of regulatory policies, including environmental policies, and it should not be a surprise that the implementation of regulatory responsibilities will change over time with the broader policy and ideological views of different administrations. Characterizing the exercise of this discretion as deregulation is not productive— better to call it inadequate, excessive, or ineffective regulation, as the case may be.

Quality and Safety Regulation. Perhaps the most controversial areas of federal regulation are the statutes and the agencies responsible for regulating the quality and safety of products and services and regulating and enforcing workplace safety. The continuing interaction between administrative regulation and tort litigation further complicates the situation.

The behavior and performance of the agencies with discretion over quality and safety are among the least studied over the past decade (Viscusi 2006 and Sunstein 2002 are exceptions) and are also the most susceptible to wide variations in implementation strategies, as well as to stealth deregulation. While the federal government has been engaged in quality and safety regulation for many years (the Food and Drug Administration, for example, was created in 1906), its responsibilities increased significantly during the 1930s and again in the 1970s. We now have a long list of federal and complementary state regulatory agencies responsible for product quality and for product and workplace safety. They include the consumer protection bureau of the Federal Trade Commission, the Consumer Product Safety Commission, the Food and Drug Administration, the National Highway Traffic Safety Administration, the Occupational Safety and Health Administration, and the Nuclear Regulatory Commission, among others. Few of these agencies have ever received high marks for their efficiency or effectiveness in actually improving product quality and product and workplace safety (Joskow and Noll 1981; Viscusi 2006), let alone consumer or worker welfare. Their role has been further complicated in some cases by controversies over the respective roles of administrative regulation and tort litigation.

While the mission statements of these agencies are sometimes broad and bold, it is often unclear exactly what metrics should be applied to measure their success in achieving them. Exactly how do we measure the effects of these agencies' efforts to regulate quality and safety? It is not clear. Have reduced budgets and staffing and the issuance of new standards by these agencies led to significant declines in safety? This is far from obvious.

While the readily available evidence is limited, most of the available indicators are positive. For example, we know that commercial aircraft fatality rates have continued to decline from very low levels over the past eight years, traffic fatality rates have been roughly constant since 2000 and roughly half what they were in 1980 (except for motorcycle rider death rates, which have increased), mine fatalities have declined, and citations and fines for mine safety violations have increased. Railroad-related injuries and fatalities have declined since 2000. Inspections by the Occupational Safety and Health Administration (OSHA) have been roughly constant, while mine inspections have decreased.

Early criticisms of the safety agencies, however, indicated that they focused too much on inspections and not enough on safety standards that would make a difference, so perhaps inspection statistics are not a good metric. Occupational deaths have declined by 62 percent and occupational injuries by 42 percent since 1971 (when OSHA was created), and fatality rates continued to decline in the past decade. How much of that improvement is due to the activities of OSHA and companion state regulatory agencies and how much to other factors (for example, changes in the structure of the U.S. economy, automobile and truck safety standards, and other factors) is not known. Moreover, fatality rates for self-employed workers, who generally fall under OSHA's radar, are much higher than for other workers, and transportation-related injuries accounted for over 40 percent of the total work-related injuries in 2007.

Fundamentally, it is hard to regulate product quality and product and workplace safety well. More than 15,000 product categories are subject to the jurisdiction of the Consumer Product Safety Commission, and millions of workplaces and thousands of job categories are covered by OSHA regulations. Consumers and workers have diverse preferences regarding risk, product quality, tradeoffs between cost and quality, tradeoffs between wages and safety, and the like. Consumers and workers may easily misestimate the risks they face and be more risk-averse than is "rational" (Sunstein 2002). Regulators must naturally focus their attention on the areas where they perceive product quality and safety issues to be very serious *and* where regulatory requirements will be effective. Riding a bicycle, skiing, climbing a ladder, riding a motorcycle, and so on will inevitably lead to accidents. A regulator can set standards for bicycle helmets but cannot force riders to wear them. Moreover, in coming to regulatory decisions, assumptions must be made about the information available to consumers, how they process it, and how it affects their behavior. Psychology and behavioral economics have something to teach in this area, but it is unclear that these agencies have ever made much effort to integrate such considerations into their regulatory procedures.

Regulation of product quality and safety can also be excessively costly to consumers, workers, and producers. Delaying the availability of new products until they meet safety and quality standards that require lengthy review procedures, for example, may be costly to consumers. This criticism has been made in the past of the Food and Drug Administration and other safety regulatory agencies that must certify products before they are released. Regulatory costs and delays may also reduce incentives to develop new products. Another criticism of health and safety regulation is that regulators are too cautious in evaluating risk and impose costs on products and workplaces that well-informed consumers and workers would not willingly bear (Viscusi 2006).

I do not think the regulation-versus-deregulation debate over product quality and product and workplace safety is particularly productive. Rather, I think it is time to go back to the beginning and clearly identify the relevant market imperfections, estimate their social costs, and examine alternative mechanisms for regulation, such as setting standards, providing information, and requiring disclosure. We should also integrate new learning from psychology and behavioral economics into the design of information and disclosure plans, so that new learning can help consumers and workers make wiser decisions and more effectively balance the costs and benefits of alternative regulatory procedures and mechanisms. In that way, we can decide whether we will rely on *regulatory actions* or on *litigation*—but not both—to provide safety and quality incentives to producers and employers.

Some Thoughts on Financial Market Regulation

I began by observing that the current financial market crisis was clearly caused by a combination of public policy failures, reinforced by behavioral failures of private sector financial institutions, intermediaries, rating agencies, creditors, and borrowers. My own view, however, is that we still do not fully understand the public policy and private sector failures and the interactions among them that caused the problems. We necessarily know even less about the appropriate public policies and private sector institutional reforms to keep these problems from emerging again.

Approaching Reform. I believe that the basic market-failures-versus-regulatory-failures framework can and should be applied to fundamental reforms of financial market regulatory institutions. I also believe that characterizing the public policy challenge as regulation versus deregulation is not particularly constructive. Finally, the lessons learned from applying this framework empirically to other areas of government regulation by microeconomists can usefully inform the evaluation of alternative potential reforms of financial market regulation. While I must leave the development of a new regulatory framework for financial markets and financial products to others with more expertise in the structure, behavior, and performance of contemporary financial market institutions, I offer the following observations based on experience with regulatory reform in other industry contexts.

Understanding the Meltdown. We must start by fully understanding what attributes of modern financial markets led to the recent meltdown and identify the most important market and institutional imperfections that led to it. The problems here are unlikely to be the new financial instruments that have been introduced in the past several years per se, but rather the private and public governance arrangements in which they are traded. Many of these innovative financial products can help diversify risks and reduce the cost of capital if they are traded within a suitable framework of public regulation and private financial firm governance. Mortgage-backed securities and other types of "simple" asset-backed securities have been around for a long time and, in principle, can help reduce risk by aggregating mortgages and similar financial assets from many different asset owners and locations facing risks that are not highly correlated. Collateralized debt obligations, which allow such securities to be sliced into tranches with different levels of risk, can, in principle, also help diversify risk and reduce risk-bearing costs. This is exactly the way corporations with tranches of secured bonds, unsecured bonds, preferred stock, and common equity have been financed for a very long time. Nor is it a bad idea, in principle, to offer insurance to holders of both private and public debt instruments. In short, many of these products appear to have attractive efficiency-enhancing properties.

What, then, is the problem? Some of these products are also complex and increasingly nontransparent, are traded in a way that may undermine incentives to evaluate risks properly, and complicate the challenges of dealing with the systemic risks that can lead to the collapse of financial markets. These outcomes, in turn, have potentially large adverse consequences for real economies. It is therefore not the products themselves but rather the market and institutional imperfections that were created or enhanced by the proliferation of such products that are the likely source of the problem. These adverse effects are exacerbated by the globalization of financial markets and the absence of a satisfactory international regulatory framework. The focus should be on the incentive and systemic risk issues associated with the institutions and their employees that create and trade these products, not simply on the products themselves.

Preventing Further Crises. Constructive analysis of what happened, how to bring the crisis to an end, and how to keep it from happening again requires starting with the right analytical perspective. I argued earlier that credit markets are different from markets for ordinary goods and services and that regulatory reform based on analogies to ordinary goods and services could be very misleading. What, then, are the attributes of financial markets that need to be better understood so that we can formulate good policies?

First, financial markets are characterized by systemic risks of collapse, with potentially serious negative implications for the performance of the larger economy. The social costs of these systemic risks are not naturally internalized into private decisions and lead to externality problems. Concerns about bank runs, bank solvency, credit market collapses, and so on have always been the rationale for prudential regulation. The failure to integrate nonbank financial institutions—including money market funds, hedge funds, investment banks, and other intermediaries—into this prudential regulatory system is likely to prove to have been an important contributor to the problems we must now confront. Why is credit insurance any different from other types of insurance, like fire insurance? We require insurance companies to hold reserves for the latter but not for the former. Why not so for credit default swaps?

Second, illiquidity costs are another externality. These costs arise when everyone tries to get out the door at the same time, driving down the price of securities to levels below their intrinsic value if held to maturity. It is easy for many money market funds to buy and sell 1 percent of their book of business each day. It is not possible for all of them to sell 20 percent of their book of business in one day for a positive price, no matter how sound are the securities they hold.

Third, the new financial products created new opportunities to quickly lay off risks on third parties who had little understanding of the risk attributes and potential liquidity costs of the underlying securities, relying on rating agencies rather than on individual due diligence. This situation created serious moral hazard problems, facilitated by the failure of the credit rating agencies to assess risks adequately. These moral hazard problems created new challenges both for regulators and for the risk management, compensation, and governance arrangements relied on by financial firms that trade these securities.

Fourth, governance imperfections at large, complex financial institutions arose from the nature of managerial compensation arrangements that rewarded short-term profits rather than long-term returns

Fifth, sophisticated investors were not as sophisticated as the regulators, especially the SEC, had assumed. Their erroneous belief led to a failure in what was thought to be largely a self-regulating system in which the sophisticated investors effectively were assumed to police the integrity of the system and as a result, protect unsophisticated investors. Given that many sophisticated financial intermediaries failed to understand the risks they had taken on and had to turn to the federal government to keep them from failing, and that many wealthy, sophisticated individuals were burned by convicted felon Bernard Madoff, the assumption that such a self-regulating system can be relied upon must be questioned.

Sixth, the creation of large private mortgage banks that could securitize and sell complex mortgage-backed securities with implicit government guarantees led to additional moral hazard problems: privatize or don't privatize, but don't privatize with implicit open-ended government safety nets—it was the worst of both worlds.

Finally, financial markets are global markets, while regulatory institutions are primarily national or subnational (state regulation of insurance in the United States, for example). An effective regulatory framework must cover the relevant geographic markets in a consistent fashion, and we must be cautious about creating regulatory agencies with inconsistent regulatory mechanisms.

New regulatory interventions should be targeted at costly market imperfections and should use the most efficient tools available to deal with them. The current regulatory framework for prudential regulation, investor, and borrower protection regulation has evolved haphazardly over many years. It involves a complex combination of federal and state regulation of banks, insurance companies, and other financial intermediaries, as well as self-regulating institutions. It has not adapted to the globalization of financial markets. Every time a new problem has emerged, we have created a new regulatory agency (or a new law, like Sarbanes-Oxley) to deal with it rather than carefully reevaluating the entire regulatory framework. We need to start with a clean slate, carefully articulate market imperfections and the regulatory goals for dealing with them, and identify regulatory mechanisms and institutions that can address the problems most effectively. We do not want simply to throw away efficiency-enhancing financial products and institutions as a "simple" regulatory response. Rather, we want private and public governance arrangements that ensure they are used properly and do not increase systematic risks of financial market collapse.

Conclusions

The regulatory and structural reforms that have been implemented over the past thirty years have, on balance, been beneficial for the economy. There are certainly exceptions, and there is always room for improvement. The ongoing problems in financial markets and with financial market regulation should not be an excuse for throwing out good regulatory reforms with the bad. Moreover, as we consider reforms to financial market regulation and financial institutions, we can learn much by analyzing the implementation and effects of regulatory reforms in other sectors. The market-failures-versus-regulatory-failures framework is robust. Characterizing the issues as regulation versus deregulation is neither robust nor constructive. Given the attributes of financial products, markets, and public and private governance alternatives, we must focus on answering the question, "What is the best that we can do in an imperfect world?"

References

Belman, Dale, and Kristen Monaco. 2001. The Effects of Deregulation, De-unionization, Technology, and Human Capital on the Work and Work-lives of Truck Drivers. *Industrial and Labor Relations Review* 54 (2a): 502–24.

Bitzan, John, and Wesley Wilson. 2007. Industry Costs and Consolidation: Efficiency Gains and Mergers in the U.S. Railroad Industry. *Review of Industrial Organization* 30: 81–105.

Coase, Ronald. 1960. The Problem of Social Cost. *Journal of Law and Economics* 3: 1–44.

Crandall, Robert. 1991. *After the Breakup: The U.S. Telecommunications Industry in a More Competitive Era.* Washington, D.C.: Brookings Institution Press.

———, and Jerry Hausman. 2000. Competition in U.S. Telecommunications Services: Effects of the 1996 Legislation. In *Deregulation of Network Industries*, ed. Sam Peltzman and Clifford Winston. Washington, D.C.: Brookings Institution Press.

Crawford, Gregory. 2000. The Impact of the 1992 Cable Act on Household Demand and Welfare. *RAND Journal of Economics* 31 (3): 422–49.

Cuddington, John, and Zhongmin Wang. 2006. Assessing the Degree of Spot Market Integration for U.S. Natural Gas: Evidence from Daily Price Data. *Journal of Regulatory Economics* 29: 195–210.

Debande, Olivier. 1999. Privatization, Deregulation and the Labour Market. *Annals of Public and Cooperative Economics* 70 (2): 277–302.

Ellerman, Denny, Paul L. Joskow, Richard Schmalensee, Jean-Pablo Montero, and Elizabeth M. Bailey. 2000. *Markets for Clean Air: The U.S. Acid Rain Program.* Cambridge: Cambridge University Press.

Grimm, Curtis, and Clifford Winston. 2000. Competition in the Deregulated Railroad Industry: Sources, Effects and Policy Issues. In

Deregulation of Network Industries, ed. Sam Peltzman and Clifford Winston. Washington, D.C.: Brookings Institution Press.

Hausman, Jerry. 1997. Valuing the Effects of New Services in Telecommunications. In *Brookings Papers on Economic Activity: Microeconomics*, 1–54. Washington, D.C.: Brookings Institution Press.

————. 1999. The Effects of Sunk Costs on Telecommunications Regulation. In *Real Options: The New Investment Theory and Its Implications for Telecommunications*, ed. J. Alleman and E. Noam. Dordrecht, Netherlands: Kluwer Academic Publishers.

Hubbard, Thomas. 2003. Information, Decisions and Productivity: Onboard Computers and Capacity Utilization in Trucking. *American Economic Review* 93: 1328–53.

Joskow, Paul L. 1987. Contract Duration and Relationship Specific Investment: The Case of Coal. *American Economic Review* 77 (1): 168–85.

————. 2000. Deregulation and Regulatory Reform in the U.S. Electric Power Sector. In *Deregulation of Network Industries*, ed. Sam Peltzman and Clifford Winston. Washington, D.C.: Brookings Institution Press.

————. 2005. Regulation and Deregulation after 25 Years: Lessons Learned for Industrial Organization. *Review of Industrial Organization* 26: 169–93.

————. 2006. Markets for Power in the United States: An Interim Assessment. *Energy Journal* 27 (1): 1–36.

————. 2007. Regulation of Natural Monopoly. In *Handbook of Law and Economics*, ed. A. M. Polinsky and S. Shavell. Amsterdam: Elsevier.

————. 2008. Lessons Learned from Electricity Market Liberalization. *Energy Journal* (special issue): 9–42. http://econ-www.mit.edu/files/2093 (accessed June 17, 2009).

Joskow, Paul L., and A. Denny Ellerman. 2008. *The EU Emissions Trading System in Perspective.* Washington, D.C.: Pew Center for Global Climate Change.

Joskow, Paul L., and Roger Noll. 1981. Regulation in Theory and Practice: A Current Overview. In *Studies in Public Regulation*, ed. G. Fromm. Cambridge, Mass.: MIT Press.

————. 1999. The Bell Doctrine: Applications in Telecommunications, Electricity and Other Network Industries. *Stanford Law Review* 51 (5): 1249–1315.

Joskow, Paul L., and Nancy Rose. 1989. The Effects of Economic Regulation. In *Handbook of Industrial Organization*, ed. Paul Joskow and Richard Schmalensee. Vol. 2. North Holland: Amsterdam.

Joskow, Paul L., and Richard Schmalensee. 1998. The Political Economy of Market-Based Environmental Policy: The 1990 U.S. Acid Rain Program. *Journal of Law and Economics* 41 (1): 36–83.

Kahn, Alfred. 1970. *The Economics of Regulation: Principles and Institutions.* Vol. 1. New York: John Wiley and Sons.

———. 1979. Applications of Economics in an Imperfect World. *American Economic Review* 69 (2): 1–13.

Laffont, Jean-Jacques, and Jean Tirole. 1993. *The Theory of Incentives and Procurement.* Cambridge, Mass.: MIT Press.

MacAvoy, Paul. 2000. *The Natural Gas Market: Sixty Years of Regulation and Deregulation.* New Haven, Conn.: Yale University Press.

McDougall, Glen, and Alasdair Roberts. 2009. *Commercializing Air Traffic Control: Have the Reforms Worked?* Research Paper 09-11. Suffolk University Law School, Boston, Mass.

Morrison, Steven, and Clifford Winston. 2000. The Remaining Role for Government Policy in the Deregulated Airline Industry. In *Deregulation of Network Industries*, ed. Sam Peltzman and Clifford Winston. Washington, D.C.: Brookings Institution Press.

Noll, Roger. 1989. Perspectives on the Politics of Regulation. In *Handbook of Industrial Organization*, ed. Robert Willig and Richard Schmalensee, 2: 1253–87. North Holland: Amsterdam.

Nordhaus, William. 2007. A Review of the Stern Review on the Economics of Climate Change. *Journal of Economic Literature* 45 (3): 686–702.

Peltzman, Sam, and Clifford Winston, eds. 2000. *Deregulation of Network Industries.* Washington, D.C.: Brookings Institution Press.

Posner, Richard. 1971. Taxation by Regulation. *Bell Journal of Economics and Management Science* 2: 22–50.

Roberts, Marc, and Michael Spence. 1992. Effluent Charges and Licenses under Uncertainty. In *Environmental Economics: A Reader*, ed. A. Markandya and J. Richardson. New York: St. Martin's Press.

Rose, Nancy. 1987. Labor Rent Sharing and Regulation: Empirical Evidence from the Trucking Industry. *Journal of Political Economy* 95 (6): 1146–78.

Stern, Nicholas. 2007. *The Economics of Climate Change: The Stern Review.* Cambridge: Cambridge University Press.

Stigler, George. 1971. The Theory of Economic Regulation. *Bell Journal of Economics and Management Science* 2: 3–21.

Sunstein, Cass. 2002. *Risk and Reason: Safety, Law and the Environment.* Cambridge: Cambridge University Press.

Swann, Christopher, and David Loomis. 2005. Competition in Local Telecommunications. *Business Economics* 40 (2): 1–28.

U.S. Federal Communications Commission. 2000. Fact Sheet: Cable Television Information Bulletin. http://www.fcc.gov/mb/facts/csgen.html (accessed June 17, 2009).

Vachal, Kimberly, John Bitzan, Tamara Vanwechel, and Dan Vinje. 2006. Differential Effects of Rail Deregulation on U.S. Grain Shippers. *Journal of Policy Reform* 9 (2): 145–55.

Viscusi, W. Kip. 2006. Regulation of Health, Safety, and Environmental Risks. AEI-Brookings Joint Center for Regulatory Studies. Related Publication 06-11. April. http://aei-brookings.org/admin/authorpdfs/redirect-safely.php?fname=./pdffiles/phpS8.pdf (accessed June 17, 2009).

Vogelsang, Ingo. 2003. Price Regulation of Access to Telecommunications Networks. *Journal of Economic Literature* 41: 830–62.

Weitzman, Martin. 1974. Prices vs. Quantities. *Review of Economic Studies* 41 (4): 477–91.

———. 2007. A Review of the Stern Review on the Economics of Climate Change. *Journal of Economic Literature* 45 (3): 703–24.

Williamson, Oliver. 1975. *Markets and Hierarchies.* New York: Free Press.

———. 1985. *The Economic Institutions of Capitalism.* New York: Free Press.

Willig, Robert, and Richard Schmalensee, eds. 1989. *Handbook of Industrial Organization.* Vol. 2. North Holland: Amsterdam.

Winston, Clifford. 1993. Economic Deregulation: Days of Reckoning for Microeconomists. *Journal of Economic Literature* 31 (3): 1263–89.

———. 2006. *Government Failure vs. Market Failure.* Washington, D.C.: Brookings Institution Press.

About the Author

Paul L. Joskow is president of the Alfred P. Sloan Foundation and is the Elizabeth and James Killian Professor of Economics and Management at the Massachusetts Institute of Technology (MIT). Professor Joskow has been on the MIT faculty since 1972, where he has served as head of the economics department (1994–98) and director of the Center for Energy and Environmental Policy Research (1999–2007); he is presently on leave from MIT.

At MIT, Professor Joskow has been engaged in teaching and research in the areas of industrial organization, energy and environmental economics, competition policy, and government regulation of industry. He has published six books and over 125 articles and papers in these areas; his papers have appeared in the *American Economic Review, Bell Journal of Economics, Rand Journal of Economics, Journal of Political Economy, Journal of Law and Economics, Journal of Law, Economics and Organization, International Economic Review, Review of Economics and Statistics, Journal of Econometrics, Journal of Applied Econometrics, Yale Law Journal, New England Journal of Medicine, Foreign Affairs, Energy Journal, Electricity Journal, Oxford Review of Economic Policy,* and other journals and books.

Professor Joskow is a director of Exelon Corporation, a director of TransCanada Corporation, and a trustee of the Putnam Mutual Funds. He is a trustee of Yale University, and served as president of the Yale University Council from 1993 to 2006. Professor Joskow has served on the U.S. Environmental Protection Agency's Acid Rain Advisory Committee and on the Environmental Economics Com-mittee of the EPA's Science Advisory Board. He is a member of the Scientific Advisory Board of the Institut d'Économie Industrielle and the Fondation Jean-Jacques Laffont (Toulouse, France).

Professor Joskow is a past president of the International Society for New Institutional Economics, a distinguished fellow of the Indus-trial Organization Society, a fellow of the Econometric Society and of the American Academy of Arts and Sciences, and a member of the Council on Foreign Relations. Professor Joskow received a BA from Cornell University in 1968 and a PhD in Economics from Yale University in 1972.

REG-MARKETS CENTER
AEI Center for Regulatory and Market Studies

The Reg-Markets Center focuses on understanding and improving regulation, market performance, and government policy. The Center provides analyses of key issues aimed at improving decisions in the public, private, and not-for-profit sectors. It builds on the success of the AEI-Brookings Joint Center for Regulatory Studies. The views expressed in this publication are those of the author.

ROBERT HAHN
Executive Director

Publications can be found at: www.reg-markets.org